Martha Stewart

A Little Go

By Judy Katschke

Illustrated by Janie Secker

A GOLDEN BOOK • NEW YORK

Educators and librarians, for a variety of teaching tools, visit us at RHTeachersLibrarians.com
Library of Congress Control Number: 2023951460
ISBN 978-0-593-71024-1 (trade) — ISBN 978-0-593-71025-8 (ebook)
Printed in the United States of America
10 9 8 7 6 5 4 3 2 1

Martha Stewart is America's first woman billionaire who built her own business. Her name is on everything, including cookware and towels, books and art supplies, and even puppy shampoo.

Martha Stewart was born Martha Helen Kostyra on August 3, 1941. The Kostyras were a hardworking Polish American family. They lived in Nutley, New Jersey, where their cozy home would become a full house—Martha was the second of six children!

All the Kostyra kids were expected to help around the house. Martha and her mother shared a name and a love of cooking. Big Martha, as she was called, taught her children how to make traditional Polish dishes like hearty stuffed cabbage, pierogi, and spice cake.

With the help of her immigrant grandmother, Martha and her brothers and sisters learned the art of canning and how to keep food fresh. Martha's father had a passion for gardening. Before long, growing plants and flowers became one of Martha's passions, too.

There was a lot to learn in the Kostyra house, and Martha loved learning. She was also a perfectionist—making sure she did everything just right!

With five brothers and sisters, Martha often had to share her toys, clothes, and books. To buy things for herself, ten-year-old Martha started babysitting after school to earn money. She looked after kids in the neighborhood, including those of famous baseball player Mickey Mantle! She also helped plan birthday parties, something Martha discovered she loved doing.

When Martha was fifteen, she began working as a model. She appeared in fashion shows and TV commercials. Martha worked just as hard in school as she did after school—she was a straight-A student!

After graduating high school, Martha packed her bags and headed to New York City to attend Barnard College of Columbia University. She loved college life. Her favorite classes were literature, art, and economics.

Martha continued modeling to earn money for her college tuition. She never thought she was glamorous, but the cameras sure did! Her smiling face was seen in fashion ads, magazines, and even a TV commercial for soap.

In 1961, Martha went on a blind date with a law student named Andy Stewart. It was love at first sight! At the end of that same year, wearing a wedding dress she sewed with her mother, Martha Kostyra became Martha Stewart.

Martha earned her college degree in 1963. Two years later, she became a mom to a baby daughter, Alexis.

Martha stopped modeling and got a job as a stockbroker. A stockbroker buys and sells shares in the ownership of companies. Martha was the only woman working at the firm—and one of the most successful women in the business at that time! After working on Wall Street for seven years, Martha decided it was time for something new.

By now, Martha and her family had moved to an old farmhouse in Westport, Connecticut. Martha got right to work fixing up what was once an onion farm. She and Andy planted many types of trees and flowers. Martha started a vegetable garden. She built a greenhouse and a barn.

The house was called Turkey Hill, but she had around eighty chickens! Martha loved caring for them and using their eggs in her recipes. And, of course, she built the chicken coop!

Inside, Martha made sure to have an extra-large kitchen with a dining area. Martha's home was the perfect place to start a catering business. She made all the food from scratch for unforgettable parties and events, and also taught cooking classes.

Martha had discovered her dream job at her dream house. It's no wonder Turkey Hill is where she first said . . .

Martha loved teaching, but not everyone could take her classes at Turkey Hill. To reach cooks everywhere, Martha decided to write a cookbook! She collected hundreds of recipes from her years of catering and added tips on flower arranging, party decorations, and even how to plan a backyard wedding.

Entertaining went on sale in 1982. The book was a big hit, and it helped make Martha Stewart a household name.

In 1990, the first issue of *Martha Stewart Living* magazine hit newsstands and mailboxes. As editor-in-chief, Martha was in charge of all the content, including her Good Things column, where she shared tips on cleaning, decorating, cooking, and organizing.

Fans really enjoyed Martha's calendar page, which had her personal appointments and scheduled projects filled in. Only Martha would have chores like "organize ice cubes," "dust books," and "order new chicks for the chicken coop"!

Martha became a popular guest on daytime TV shows. Then, in 1993, she got her own show! Many episodes were filmed right in her home. What better place for Martha to cook her mother's meatloaf, carve a pumpkin, and decorate a barn door?

Martha's personal life wasn't always as perfect as it seemed.

Her marriage to Andy ended, and in 2004, she was found guilty of committing a financial crime. Martha was sentenced to five months at a prison camp in West Virginia. While there, she mopped the floors and cleaned the bathrooms. There was nothing good about prison, but Martha made the best of her time by exercising, making friends with other inmates, and crafting. Everyone was impressed with the nativity set she made in pottery class!

When her prison sentence ended, Martha boarded a plane wearing a poncho crocheted by a fellow inmate. She returned to her house with plans to never look back, only forward. And what was she most looking forward to that first night home? Making risotto for dinner!

Martha got right back to work. She wrote more books and magazines, starred in more TV shows, and made a new best friend: the rapper Snoop Dogg.

When she's not working or hanging out with Snoop Dogg, Martha likes spending time with her pet dogs. Over the years, she has had many fluffy chow chows and little French bulldogs.

Ever since she was a little girl, Martha always worked hard to do her best. And if life threw her lemons, Martha made lemonade—with pureed strawberries and sparkling seltzer water!

Thanks to her magazines, TV shows, and many books—she's written more than ninety!—Martha Stewart has helped people everywhere make their homes and lives more beautiful. And that, as she might say, is a *very* good thing!